BUDDHA

BUDDHA

Joan Lebold Cohen

ILLUSTRATED BY

Mary Frank

MACDONALD : LONDON

To my
earthly attachments

JERRY

PETER

SETH

ETHAN

Contents

1. CONCEPTION AND BIRTH   11

2. PRINCE SIDDARTHA'S CHILDHOOD   19

3. RENUNCIATION: SIDDARTHA LEAVES
   HIS FAMILY AND KINGDOM   31

4. GOTAMA THE ASCETIC SEARCHES
   FOR ENLIGHTENMENT   37

5. ENLIGHTENMENT   47

6. THE BUDDHA   55

7. THE FINAL DAYS   71

   Glossary   77

   Epilogue   83

BUDDHA

1. Conception and Birth

More than two thousand years ago in the foothills of the Himalaya Mountains there lived a King, Suddhodhana. He was the chief of the Sakya clan and, from his capital Kapilavastu, he ruled justly and well. King Suddhodhana was one of a long line of rulers of the Sakya clan, whose ancestors went back to the time the earth was created. His wife, Queen Maya, came from a kingdom not far away.

In the year 568 B.C. the King proclaimed that the summer Moon Festival should be celebrated in his realm. In honour of the festival the Queen bathed in perfumed water, made garlands of coloured flowers, and gave 400,000 gold pieces to the poor. She dressed herself in state robes of the finest silk finished with gold and silver threads. She dined on a banquet of exquisite delicacies, and afterwards lay down to rest in the richly adorned state bed chamber. Then she had a dream.

In her dream four great kings lifted her bed, carried her through the air to the Himalayas, and placed her beneath a great Sal tree seven leagues high. The four queens of the four kings came to bathe her and dress her in heavenly clothing, anoint her with perfume, and adorn her with garlands of flowers. Then they led her to a golden palace at the top of a silver mountain. There she reclined on a jewelled bed. Soon a white elephant appeared. His silvery trunk held a white lotus flower, and he trumpeted as he entered the palace. He circled Queen Maya's bed three times and then touched her right side.

When the Queen awoke she told the King her dream. The King summoned 64 Brahmans, the wisest priests in his Kingdom. He invited them to join in a banquet and offered them gifts. Then the King told these wise men of Queen Maya's dream and asked if they would interpret it. The Brahmans said, "Do not worry. The Queen has conceived a male child, and you will have a son. If he

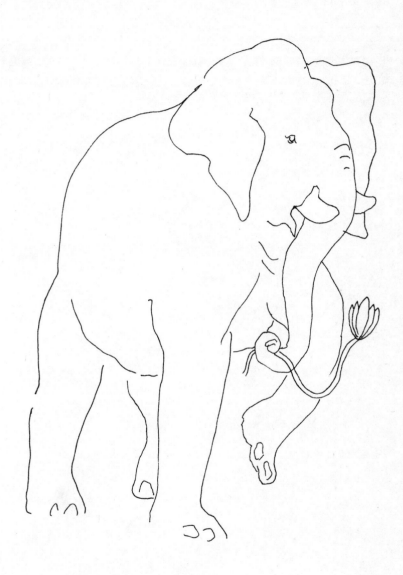

lives in this house, he will become King. If he leaves this house and goes forth into the world, he will understand suffering and find salvation. If he does this, he will become the greatest prophet the earth will know for hundreds of thousands of years."

Meanwhile there had been a violent earthquake accompanied by 32 signs from heaven. There seemed to be boundless light which made the blind see again. The deaf could hear; the lame could walk.

Queen Maya had conceived and was to bear a child within the magical forecast of ten lunar months. In her pregnancy she became round and full. As the time approached to deliver the child, the Queen asked the King if she might return to her family home at Devadaha for the birth. The King agreed and ordered the road to be smoothed and adorned with vessels full of plantains, a variety of bananas, and decorated with bright silk banners which fluttered in the balmy breezes from the hills. The Queen set out in a palanquin, a golden carrying chair, accompanied by a retinue of a thousand courtiers.

Halfway between the two cities was a grove of Sal trees, known as the Lumbini Garden. It was blanketed with flowers, and birds and bees flew and sang, filling the air with garden music. When the

Queen saw this grove, she wanted to stop and rest. She walked to the foot of a great Sal tree and reached up, wishing to hold one of its branches. The branch bent down to meet her hand. She grasped it, and at that moment, miraculously, the baby was born out of her right side. Four goddesses received the baby in a golden net—he was shining and perfect. They presented him to his mother and said, "Rejoice Queen, a mighty son has been born to you." Just then two streams of water descended from heaven, one hot and one cold, so that the mother and child could be refreshed in a ceremonial bath. The baby had a radiance dazzling as the sun, yet he attracted all eyes as does the moon. The four great kings, guardians of the four directions, north, south, east, and west, held the baby on a silver pillow while gods and men came to worship and admire him and offer him garlands of flowers. They praised him saying, "Exquisite child, you are truly a prince among men." The baby was protected by an umbrella made of a lotus flower held by the admiring gods. The miraculous baby took seven steps in each direction to examine the entire universe. He then declared in a voice like the roar of a lion, "I will bring new understanding to the world and be the saviour. I will find the way to end suffering on earth."

The day that the baby was born there were many

other important events: a Bo tree seedling sprouted that would grow into the tree of enlightenment; his future wife, who would be mother of his son, was born and so was his half-brother Ananda the Fair. And on that same day, an elephant, horse, and charioteer were born, all of whom would play an important role in his life.

Queen Maya and the baby, Prince Siddartha, were taken back to Kapilavastu.

On the day of the birth, Asita, an aged and wise sage who lived high in the Himalayas, saw the gods in the sky as they rejoiced over the great event. Learning the cause of their joy through these celestial signs, Asita descended from the mountains and went to see the marvellous child. At the palace of King Suddhodhana he was graciously received. Asita saw the shining boy, who was adorned with the thirty-two marks of wisdom that appear on those destined to be great men. The most obvious of these were a bump on the top of his head, a mole between his eyebrows, and lotus buds and wheels on the palms of his hands and the soles of his feet. Asita admired the child and said to the King, "If he lives in this house, he will become King. If he goes forth from here to live without a house or kingdom, he will become the Buddha, removing the veil of ignorance from the world." But then the great sage began to weep and sigh.

The King asked Asita why he wept. Was there a misfortune in the boy's future? Asita answered, "No, King, I do not weep for the boy. I weep for myself. I am old and when the boy becomes the Buddha I will be gone from this life and will not be able to honour him and learn from him."

2. Prince Siddartha's Childhood

Queen Maya was filled with both joy and fear after the birth of her marvellous child. Her joy was a mother's natural joy, but her fear stemmed from the extraordinary prophecies made about her son. Quite exhausted by these events, seven days after Siddartha was born, Queen Maya died. The little

19

prince was tenderly mothered by his aunt, Prajapati, who had given birth to a son named Nanda
on the same day Queen Maya had borne Siddartha. Siddartha and his half-brother Nanda were
brought up like twins with all the luxuries of King
Suddhodhana's peaceful and prosperous court.
There were thirty-two nurses to attend to their
every need and amuse them day and night.

Young Prince Siddartha, perfect as the morning
sun shining on the mountain, was given three pal-
aces in which to live: one for the cold season, one
for the hot, and one for the rainy season. His
father had three lotus pools made for his pleasure:
one was filled with white lotus flowers, another
with red lotuses, and the third with blue lotuses.
He was given furniture made of sweet-smelling
sandalwood from Benares, and his princely clothing was woven by the finest weavers, from the
most perfect threads, also from Benares. He was
protected from sun, wind, and rain by a white
parasol, ate only the most delicate foods, and was
entertained each day by a vast retinue of beautiful
women who played golden tambourines and
danced with the grace of angels.

When Siddartha was thirteen years old, the King
took him to a festival to celebrate the beginning of
the ploughing season. There were a thousand

ploughs: 891 wooden ploughs for the peasants, 108 silver ploughs for the courtiers, and a golden plough for the King. Prince Siddartha sat down under a rose-apple tree at the beginning of the contest, assuming the position of meditation, his legs crossed, soles of the feet up. He saw the plough turn up a frog and a serpent from the soil. The frog would be eaten by men and the serpent thrown away. This puzzled Siddartha and made him think about how some living things are consumed and others discarded. Contemplating this, he fell into a trance. After the ploughing contest, when it was time for the feast to begin, the courtiers looked around for Siddartha. They discovered him still in a trance under the rose-apple tree, and they saw that the shadow of the tree which protected the Prince from the morning sun had not moved throughout the day. The courtiers rushed to the King to report the event, and the King understood it to be another sign of his son's remarkable destiny.

When the Prince was sixteen, King Suddhodhana sent messages to the members of his family in the Sakya clan declaring that Siddartha was now a man, ready to marry, and that he would give the Prince a Kingdom. "Let all send their daughters. Siddartha is ready to choose a wife," the King said. The clan members retorted, "He is handsome, but he does not know how to protect himself and his family in case of war." And so, the Prince had to prove that he was skilled in the manly arts.

King Suddhodhana proclaimed seven days of athletic contests. These tournaments would pit the skill of all the young men of the Sakya clan against Prince Siddartha. There were contests in running, jumping, fencing, wrestling, and the favoured sport, archery. Siddartha defeated his rivals easily in the first four events. His wrestling opponents fell like straw from a flick of his wrist. Finally, the archery contest began. As the event progressed, the targets were moved farther and farther away from the archers. At last it was Siddartha's turn. He took up a bow and drew it, but it snapped in his powerful hands. He asked for a stronger bow. The King said there was one used by his grandfather, but since his death, no one had been able even to lift or to string it. People said that it would take a thousand men to draw it. The bow was brought to the Prince, who strung it with his toe, plucked the bow string until it sounded like thunder, and drew it with ease. Every shot hit the exact centre of the target in such a way that each arrow pierced the one before it.

Devadatta, a cousin of the Prince, also participated in the contest. He wounded one of the royal

geese and wanted to kill it. But Siddartha picked up the bird and bound its lame wing, leaving Devadatta in a rage. From then on, this cruel cousin was jealous of Siddartha's power. Devadatta would even try to kill the Buddha.

Now Prince Siddartha had proved his skill in the arts of war. The noblemen of the Sakya clan dressed each of their daughters in her finest robes and jewels and offered her to the Prince in marriage. One by one, on the appointed day, they were introduced to the Prince. He presented a jewel to each maiden, but no one was brave enough to look him in the eye, so he was not impressed. Now there were no more jewels to give, but one last maiden, who was as fragile and tender as a young bud beginning the perfection of her bloom, had yet to be presented to the Prince. She, Yasodhara, was able to look Siddartha in the eye without embarrassment. Yasodhara asked the Prince if she had done something to displease him and if this was the reason that she did not receive a jewel. The Prince took off his ring and presented it to her. She said she could not accept the ring because she did not wish to deprive him of his adornments. Rather, she wished to become an adornment to him. So he chose this last graceful maiden, Yasodhara, to be his bride, and she would become the mother of his child, Rahula. They were married according to the ancient rites and customs of the Sakya clan, by joining hands and circling a holy fire three times. After the wedding feast a splendid procession, led by courtiers, made its way to Prince Siddartha's palace. He went on horseback, while his delicate bride was carried in a palanquin with many attendants. In her retinue were ladies-in-waiting wearing jewels that tinkled as they moved as well as musicians playing tambourines, drums, and bells.

The young Prince and Princess amused themselves with innumerable wedding gifts. There were couches covered with exquisitely embroidered silk, rugs bright as an indoor garden, sweet smelling perfumes, and garlands of flowers. Each palace had gardens in which they could play games and devote themselves to all sorts of pleasures. These were embellished with pools of the coolest water to refresh the body and spirit. Each palace also had entertainers, dancers, singers, and storytellers. Musicians played upon flutes, and harps, and the vina, a favourite instrument of both gods and men. King Suddhodhana gave all this to amuse and occupy his son, hoping that he would become the monarch and continue the line of Sakya kingship. He wanted to protect his son from any ugliness in life, hoping that by sheltering him in this way, Siddartha would not leave his Kingdom as the prophecy had fore-told.

One day Prince Siddartha called his charioteer to take him to the park. The King ordered that the road be cleared of all but beautiful sights and the golden chariot be harnessed to four of the finest horses and decorated with lotus petals like a vehicle of the gods. The Prince paraded through the streets of the city. All the women crowded onto their balconies to throw flowers in his path. Past the city gates on the royal highway, a god, disguised as an old man, appeared before the chariot. This wrinkled old man was worn-out with age. His crooked body was supported by a stick held in his trembling hand. He had white hair and no teeth. The Prince, puzzled, asked the charioteer what sort of man this was. The charioteer replied that all men must endure old age, and that even Sid-dartha himself would not be spared. At that the Prince forgot his lighthearted visit to the park and became lost in thought about the fact that every-one must grow old.

A few days later, the Prince again summoned his charioteer to take him to the park. The King re-peated the order that nothing unpleasant should offend the Prince's sight. The road was cleared and the chariot readied, but again the gods contrived to open Siddartha's eyes. Just beyond the western city gate he saw a sick man who was suffering great pain. Again Siddartha forgot his pleasure and thought about pain and suffering in the world.

On the third trip to the park the gods contrived that the Prince should come across a funeral procession. There was a dead man wrapped in a shroud and laid on a pyre of wood, about to be cremated; his family and friends were weeping, moaning, and beating their breasts. From then on, Siddartha was no longer able to think of anything but man's fate. He knew that all who were born would suffer. He knew that all beings who are born must bear old age and sickness and death. How could he ever again pursue pleasure with this knowledge?

On another day when he tried to return to the park, Siddartha and his charioteer met an ascetic, a holy man who had abandoned his home and possessions and who wandered from place to place silently begging for food. This ascetic had left his wife and family and was now at home in the great deserts and forests. His eyes seemed to express that he was at peace with himself and his fate. Siddartha was impressed by the humility and bearing of the man. The charioteer, inspired by the gods, told Siddartha of the virtues of renunciation. He explained that a life of comfort and pleasure would not lead to an understanding of man's suffering. If, however, he would leave his family and kingdom to meditate, free from the ties of his life of pleasure, he might find an escape from suffering. Siddartha thought about this and knew that he must renounce his princely life.

Now Siddartha's day of renunciation had arrived. He was bathing in the park when news was brought that a son had been born to him. Both father and mother were delighted and the Prince named the boy Rahula. But the joyous event of Rahula's birth did not sway Siddartha's decision. That day, he had resolved to renounce his crown and family in search of enlightenment. He would give up his own pleasure so that he could understand the causes of suffering in the world and find the way to overcome it.

3. Renunciation: Siddartha Leaves his Family and Kingdom

That night, while everyone was asleep, Prince Siddartha went to his father's palace and stood silently next to the sleeping King. King Suddhodhana was awakened by a brilliant light. He called his guard to ask if the sun had risen. The guard answered that it was midnight with half the night still to go before sunrise. Then the King realized that the radiance shone forth from his son, Prince Siddartha. The Prince begged his father to bless him and not to stand in the way of his departure from his family and kingdom. The King wept and promised to give Siddartha all that he possessed if only he would stay. The Prince replied that he would stay if his father would promise that Siddartha would be exempt from old age, sickness, and death. Since the King was unable to grant this to him, he could not oppose his son's destiny.

When the Prince returned to his own palace, it was as though he had never left. All were in a deep sleep inspired by the gods. As he gazed upon the motionless musicians, dancers, and the ladies of the harem who created this illusion of a life of pleasure, he knew that they too would become old and die, and he repeated his vow to leave his palace for a homeless life. He went to his son, Rahula, who was sleeping with his mother, Yasodhara, on a bed strewn with sweet-smelling jasmine flowers. The mother's hand lay on her son's head. Siddartha watched and thought that if he moved Yasodhara's hand in order to take his son, she would awaken and try to prevent his departure. So he decided that he would return for his son after he had become the Buddha.

Siddartha mounted his horse, and his charioteer clung to the horse's tail in order to accompany his master. The gods held their hands under the horse's hooves to muffle the noise of departure. King Suddhodhana had tripled the guards at all the gates in an effort to stop the Prince, but the

guards, like everyone else in Kapilavastu that night, were drugged in a celestial sleep, and the god who dwelt in the city gate opened it for the blessed party.

Just then, Mara, god of evil, appeared in Siddartha's path. He said, "Stay! If you do, in seven days I will give you the universe as your empire. You will rule over the four great islands and the two hundred smaller ones. Turn back!" Siddartha refused. Mara was furious that he was unable to tempt the Prince away from his righteous quest. He threatened Siddartha and promised to follow his every footstep.

There was a full moon on this night when the Prince gave up his luxurious life. As he left the city the Prince felt a surging desire to look back, a sign that he might be losing his determination to give up life's pleasures and comforts. Again the gods helped. They turned the earth around, so that when he looked back he saw nothing.

The gods accompanied the Prince as he travelled thirty leagues beyond the three Kingdoms. When he reached a great river, he crossed it in one leap. On the other side, he stopped, took off his jewels, and gave them to his charioteer. Shortly afterwards the noble party encountered a huntsman. Siddartha exchanged his princely robes for the huntsman's tattered coat. Then he grasped his scimitar in one hand and his topknot of hair in the other and cut off his princely locks. For ever after, his hair would curl to the right, a hair's breadth from his head.

The next morning in Kapilavastu all the people were uneasy. During the night there had been shattering earthquakes as a sign from the vanquished Mara, and of course the Prince was nowhere to be found. The King ordered a party to search for him. Following the Prince's footprints, which were in the form of sacred lotus flowers, they found the horse and the charioteer who had carried the Prince's golden ornaments. The King thought the Prince had been killed and robbed of his precious jewellery. The charioteer told of Prince Siddartha's departure and his resolve to abandon the world and become an ascetic. The Prince had vowed to maintain a religious life and had cut off his hair, cast off his princely robes, and set forth into a homeless existence. No longer would he be Prince Siddartha. From that moment he would be "Gotama the Ascetic." The gods then left Gotama, to let him seek his own enlightenment.

4. Gotama the Ascetic Searches for Enlightenment

Gotama the Ascetic began his journey by following the course of the Ganges River as it flows south and east from the Himalayas, watering the vast parched plains on its way to the great ocean. He sought out Brahman teachers and lived with them to learn the rites and practices of the priesthood. He quickly mastered the prayers and discovered that he could perform the ritual from memory, but this, he found, led neither to his understanding

37

nor his enlightenment. Gotama soon left the Brahman priests and continued his dusty journey along the banks of the Ganges.

After spending the night on a mountain near a city built on five hills, famous for its natural hot springs, he entered the city through the gate of hot waters and walked with his begging bowl in hand. The people noticed this handsome ascetic with his majestic bearing, composed expression, and glowing complexion, and a crowd began to follow him. That evening Gotama retired to the mountain from whence he had come. The king of that city heard of this remarkable monk and went up to visit him the next day. In order to see the monk, he had to leave his chariot and walk on the stony hillside. The King was so impressed by the monk's countenance that he bowed down to him and offered him half of his throne. Gotama refused the King's gracious offer, but promised to return when he had attained enlightenment and share the secret of salvation with the King. So the King might also become enlightened. Then Gotama resumed his journey.

Some leagues later he approached a master named Rudraka, who was preaching to seven hundred disciples. Gotama joined this holy man in order to learn what he could about the causes and cures of suffering. Rudraka taught him the

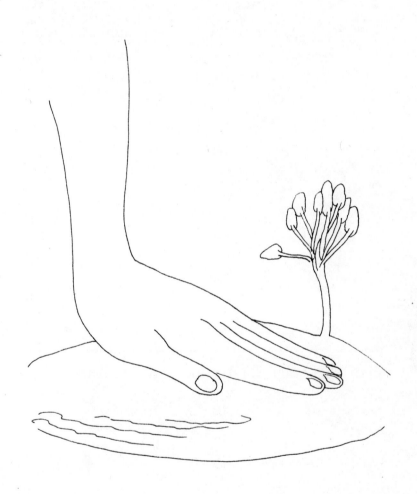

positions for meditation, breathing exercises, mental concentration, and physical privation, so that the disciple could completely control his body and mind. These methods would put the disciple into a trance, leading him to unite with a deity. Gotama soon saw that Rudraka's teaching would not answer his questions about man's suffering so he left the master to seek his own path of enlightenment. Five disciples joined him, and they wandered further down the Ganges over rocky hillsides and across rich valleys. They stopped when they saw the clear waters of the Nairanjana River and its peaceful wooded banks. Here was the place to begin their meditation.

For six years they practised the severest sort of asceticism. They believed that by making the mind the master of the body, they could endure incredible physical hardship and thus forget the body's pain and pleasure. Then they would begin to comprehend the unknowable. The idea of ignoring the flesh to the point of torturing it was an old one in India. Many holy men practised this discipline hoping that it would enable them to understand more of man and the cosmos.

Gotama the Ascetic underwent three forms of discipline. The first test involved physical posture. For six years he sat on the earth with his legs crossed, the soles of his feet turned upwards to the sky, and the palms of his hands turned up on his lap. He made his mind the master of his body. He held his posture through wind and rain, sun and moon, hot and cold. He controlled his trembling and kept his limbs absolutely erect while sweat poured from his body. At the end of the sixth year he stopped breathing. A noise crashed in his ears as if the surf were pounding on a rocky coast, and his head was racked with pain as though giant hailstones were falling on it. The gods feared that Gotama was dead, and so did his mother, Queen Maya, who saw all this from Tusita Heaven, the blissful resting spot where she awaited rebirth. She wept for her son. But this was only the first of Gotama's trials.

The next step in this physical ordeal was a fast. At first he ate only one kernel of a jujube, one grain of rice, and one grain of millet. Finally, he ate nothing. His body wasted away till there was only skin covering a bony skeleton. His head looked like a withered gourd, his skin like a dried leaf about to crumble to dust.

The third hardship was not moving. While continuing his fast Gotama was committed to not moving a finger to protect himself from weather, pests, bugs, vermin, or reptiles. These physical disciplines were so great that he lost the ability to focus his eyes upon objects in front of him. The villagers who saw him as they gathered reeds and dung thought that he was a demon of dust. They jeered at him and threw dirt at him. Yet he did not move.

Gotama the Ascetic showed that he could withstand these dreadful disciplines better than anyone else, but the torture of the flesh did not lead him to enlightenment. He knew he must find another way to understand man's fate. He left his five companions, who despised him for abandoning his fast. They did not understand that he had abandoned physical privation in search of the true way to enlightenment, just as he had left the Brahman priests and Rudraka the Holyman because their paths did not lead to understanding. The same essential questions remained unanswered. There was always the same endless cycle: birth, death, and rebirth, like a wheel that never stopped turning. Suffering and pain exist within this relentless cycle. The destiny of the Buddha was to find a way to alleviate suffering by escaping the cycle of rebirth. He would lift the veil of ignorance and show the way to salvation.

Having abandoned the extremely austere life, Gotama now felt he must clothe himself, so he took the linen shroud of a dead woman to wear as a mantle. Before wearing it he had to wash away the impurity of death. He needed water and a stone to scrub the linen. He found a stone but no water, so he struck the ground with the palms of his hands, and water came from the earth, forming a pond. Thereafter, that pond was called "struck-by-the-Hand." Gotama went into the pond to wash the shroud, but he was so weak that he could not get out of the water without the aid of a tree spirit, a Yakshi, who offered her branch and helped him out. A young woman who lived near the pond saw Gotama and filled a bowl with rice and sour milk for him so that he might regain his strength after his fast.

Now Gotama took his linen and went to the Nairanjana River to bathe and purify himself. The river was extraordinarily beautiful, clear and cool, with a sandy bottom that pleased the feet of the blessed bather. The river god and his bride came to greet Gotama, praise him, and shower him with perfumed flowers. They knew that after this purification would come the final step toward enlightenment.

Gotama cleaned and clothed himself and ate the rice and milk which restored his physical beauty. He set out towards Bodhgaya to find the spot where he would finally understand suffering, thus lifting the veil of ignorance for the world. The night before he reached the appointed site, he had a dream. He dreamed that the earth was a great couch on which he reclined, with the Himalayas as a pillow. His left hand was plunged into the eastern ocean, his right hand into the western ocean, and his feet into the southern ocean. This was a sign that his moment of triumph was at hand.

5. Enlightenment

The next morning Gotama walked near a grove of Sal trees, where he met a humble grass cutter. The grass cutter offered him some fresh-cut bundles. Gotama took the grass and spread it out to make a fresh and pure seat at the foot of the Bodhi tree. He sat in a yoga position on the grass beneath the tree, his legs crossed and the soles of his feet turned upwards on the top of his thighs. He vowed that he would sit on that seat even if his body dried up and his flesh dissolved; that he would not move from there until he had achieved enlightenment.

Thus Gotama began the final stage of his journey toward understanding. He sat there under the Bodhi tree for forty-nine days, concentrating on man's pain and suffering. At that point Mara, god of evil, who had unsuccessfully followed Gotama for six years in the hope of catching him in an evil or unkind act, made his final assault. He attacked the defenceless ascetic with his army of demons, repulsive monsters with panting tongues, curved fangs, red burning eyes, and twisted bodies. Some of these ghastly creatures had a hundred heads to one body. Other devils were headless with a thousand arms. Some were covered with serpents who spat fire. Others made thunder by clapping their hands, and threw bolts of lightning at the motionless monk. But Gotama was protected from the forces of evil by all the good acts he had performed in this life and in his former lives. Not a hair on his body was touched. Mara urged his troops on, but the demons' weapons were turned into flowers and their spiny bodies became soft as the inside of an egg. They fled from Gotama's indestructible and shining presence and vanished back into the darkest regions.

Since this armed attack had failed miserably, Mara sent his daughters, more beautiful than any women on earth, hoping that they might be able to tempt Gotama away from his virtuous path.

Mara's exquisite daughters sang and danced before Gotama. Their glistening bodies were like heavenly instruments and they sang with such perfection that all the gods stopped to listen. But Gotama was not moved. To signal his triumph over Mara, Gotama touched the earth with his hand, calling it to bear witness to his great victory.

With Mara defeated, Gotama was able to advance to his final stages of meditation. He concentrated and directed his thoughts to his many lives before this one, and the pleasure and pain that he had suffered in each life. He understood the great cycle of rebirth, called *samsara*, which is like a wheel in perpetual motion. He remembered the countless times the earth had been destroyed and re-created in this cyclical pattern. The earth, polluted by the corruption of man, is scorched by the sun and consumed in the unthinkable heat of its flames. Then it is created again, purified and perfect, lifted from the watery depths of the endless ocean by the great creative forces of the universe. Thus the earth is created pure and innocent, just as each baby is born, and then the earth is destroyed after it has become corrupt and polluted with evil, just as all men suffer and die. Gotama reflected on this inescapable rhythm, the creation and destruction and rebirth of all living things, and their inability to escape the suffering and pain of old age, sickness, and death each time they are reborn.

Gotama then began the second stage of meditation. He thought about good deeds performed by people during their lives. He understood that if a person acted in a good and virtuous way during his lifetime, he would be reborn to an honoured position in his next life. This deserving soul might be reborn as a king or a saint, or, ultimately, a Buddha. If, however, a person behaved badly and had evil thoughts, he would be reborn into a degraded and miserable state, such as a mouse or a toad or a viper. Gotama realized that man could influence his rebirth by his behaviour in this life, and this revelation marked the second stage of understanding in his search for enlightenment.

Gotama was then ready for the third and final stage of illumination. He realized that the pain and suffering during each existence came from a person's attachments to life's pleasures such as family, possessions, and comfort. Only if a person detaches himself from these pleasures, if he withdraws from life, if he is not tempted by craving or desire for them, can he escape *samsara*, the endlessly spinning wheel of rebirth, and attain the perfect peace of *nirvana*—a stateless state, beyond *samsara*. Having attained *nirvana*, one need never be reborn and suffer again.

The enlightenment had come after fifty days under the Bodhi tree. The blessed one was no longer Gotama the Ascetic, he was now the Buddha Sakyamuni, sage of the Sakya clan, the enlightened one. He had lifted the veil of ignorance and found the path to salvation.

6. The Buddha

After attaining his goal of enlightenment, the Buddha Sakyamuni stayed on the spot of his illumination for seven days detached from the world of suffering, experiencing the peace of *nirvana*. He sat serenely, yogi style. A storm came up during his blissful meditation. But the Naga King, Muscalinda, who admired the Buddha's achievement, left his underground abode, encircled the body of the Buddha, and spread his great serpent's head like a canopy over the head of the Blessed One to protect him from the wind and rain.

The time had come for the Buddha to go forth and share his understanding, to help others towards their enlightenment. First of all, he would go to the five disciples whom he had abandoned when he had broken his fast. The Buddha would teach them his law, and they would be his first converts. After his great fast the Buddha had to eat before he began his journey. Food was offered to him by two simple merchants, but the Buddha could not accept it, since he possessed no bowl and monks are not allowed to accept food hand to hand. Once again the guardian kings of the four directions descended and offered him a begging bowl.

Sakyamuni set out towards Benares, where he knew he would find his former disciples. After several days of walking, he reached the banks of the Ganges. To go to Benares he had to cross this river, which was swollen by the melting snow of the Himalayas. Since it flowed like a torrent, he could neither swim nor hang on to the tail of a cow to cross it. The Buddha saw a ferry and asked the ferryman to take him across. When the ferryman insisted upon receiving his fare in advance, the Buddha, who had only his mantle and his empty bowl, leaped into the air and crossed the Ganges in an instant. The ferryman collapsed with horror, realizing that he had missed his opportunity to aid a saint. News of this event reached the ears of the King of Benares, who decreed that henceforth all Holymen should be ferried free.

The blessed pilgrim arrived at Sarnath, just four miles north of Benares, where his former disciples were. They were living in the Deer Park, which was to be the site of the Buddha's first sermon. The Deer Park was an especially suitable place for this historic event because of something that had happened in a former life of the Buddha.

Long ago the King of Benares had had a great zest for hunting, but there had been so much unnecessary killing that the King of the Deer had made a pact with the King of Benares. The Deer King had said he would provide one deer for the King of Benares' table every day if he would promise to stop hunting. On the first day a lottery was held to decide which deer to offer. The Sakyamuni Buddha in his former life took pity on the luckless doe that was chosen, transformed himself into her image, and took her place. When the royal chef saw this noble beast, his knife fell from his hand and he could not bring himself to kill it. The King of Benares was so moved by the Buddha's self-sacrifice that he declared that no deer should be harmed forever more. But it was not so simple; the deer were eating the peasants' crops, and the peasants refused to abide by the King's decree. So the King created the "Deer Park" for the protection of deer.

As Sakyamuni entered the Deer Park, his former disciples saw him in the distance. They agreed among themselves that they would not welcome him because they thought he had succumbed to weakness and for this reason had given up their austere fasting and discipline. But when the disciples were actually in the presence of the blessed Sakyamuni, they were overcome by a desire to welcome him and rose to their feet even though they had vowed to ignore him. One took his mantle and bowl, a second brought him a seat, while another brought water to bathe his feet. They could not help being awed by the serenity in his eyes and his shining presence.

They began to talk with Sakyamuni, who told them of his enlightenment and of how he had become the Buddha. They felt embarrassed and sorry that they had deserted him and begged his forgiveness. Then they listened while the Buddha preached his first sermon. It was called "turning the wheel of law." It taught the Buddha's middle way—the four noble truths and the eightfold path. As he preached, the disciples began to understand his doctrine.

The Buddha explained first what he meant by

the "middle way." One should not live a life devoted to the pursuit of pleasure, nor should one lead a life of extreme austerity devoted to intentionally mistreating his body. One should follow the middle course between these two extremes.

Next the Buddha proceeded to define the four noble truths. First of all, what is suffering? Suffering is birth, old age, illness, living with someone one does not love, being separated from the person one loves; in effect *all of life is suffering*.

Secondly, he stated that a person sees himself as an important being on earth, but the fact is, a person is like the smallest grain of sand at the bottom of a vast ocean. A person is unimportant in the vast cycle of recurring births of man and the universe. Man's tragic vice is his illusion that he is someone meaningful when really he is insignificant, transient, destructible, and replaceable. The craving for life is man's downfall, because *the life he clings to is an illusion*. It is because of this illusion that suffering and pain occur.

Thirdly, to escape the endless cycle of rebirth, and the desire to cling to a false existence, one must cut his ties with life which is illusion. *Only through detachment from life can one escape suffering and find salvation*.

The last of the four noble truths is a prescription for the end of pain and suffering. The Buddha

told his disciples to *follow the eightfold path.*
think right thoughts, say right words and perform
right deeds, have right aspirations and intentions,
live the right way of life, perform right efforts and
meditations. The Buddha then elaborated upon
how to follow the eightfold path.

In this first sermon the wheel of the Buddha's
law began to turn, leading others to their awakening. In the future these first five converts would
follow his middle way and the prescription for a
righteous way of life. The news of the Buddha's
enlightenment travelled fast. Aspirants from all
social classes and all stations of Indian life sought
him out in order to learn his law and find salvation. One of the first to come was the nephew of
Asita, the great sage who had forecast the Buddha's
destiny at his birth. Asita had known that he would
be dead when Sakyamuni became enlightened so
he made his nephew promise to be the Buddha's
disciple in his stead.

Soon after, thirty young men who had formed a
society dedicated to the enjoyment of life went on
a picnic in the woods. Since all the men were married save one, a girl friend was invited to keep the
bachelor company. But when the men plunged
into a woodland pond to refresh themselves, this
girl stole all the robes of the swimmers and ran
away. The men pursued her, but in their search

they came upon the Buddha. They asked whether the Buddha had seen the unscrupulous female. The Buddha replied: "Do you think, young men, it is better for you to search for the woman or to search within yourselves?" This led the men to renounce their lives of pleasure and to become his disciples. There would be many more disciples in his lifetime and even more followers after his death.

Not all the conversions went so easily. Near Sarnath, there was a Brahmanic sect, a group of holymen who lived in wooden huts at the edge of the jungle. Their chief, Kasyapa, practised an ancient religion which had a great following. Sakyamuni, pleased with his early successes in conversion and full of confidence, went to live with these Brahmans hoping to teach them his law and show them the true path to salvation. Kasyapa saw how popular the handsome ascetic was with the villagers. To remind the villagers that he, Kasyapa, was their leader who possessed great powers, he performed feats of magic. Although monks were forbidden to use magic, the Buddha realized that he too must perform magic if he were to succeed in winning over these non-believers, so he performed miracles with the elements fire and water.

Kasyapa and his holymen worshipped fire in the hearth of their sacred hut. Sakyamuni requested permission from Kasyapa to sleep in that hut with the sacred fire. Kasyapa warned him that the all-powerful Naga, who guarded the fire, would consume him, but he allowed the young ascetic to prove himself in this way. The Buddha entered the hut, and a momentous struggle followed. Huge flames accompanied by columns of black sulphurous smoke issued from the hut. But in the end the Buddha's power overwhelmed the Naga's fury and Sakyamuni emerged triumphant.

Later that year, while Sakyamuni was still living in the village, the rains came with unusual fury, causing a great flood over the countryside. Kasyapa was concerned about the young ascetic, so he set out in a boat to search for his guest. He saw the Buddha walking on the water with dry feet. It was then that Kasyapa, the aged holy man with the tousled locks, bowed his head to the Buddha, whose locks were shorn. It was customary for a priest of the old religion to wear his hair long but the Buddha had cut his hair as a symbol of the severing of all worldly ties when he left his father's house.

Stopping only during the rainy season, Sakyamuni continued his wanderings and made converts along the way. He taught his followers to do the same. One of the places to which he journeyed was the city of five hills with springs of hot waters. He had promised its King that after achieving enlightenment he would return there to share the secret of salvation.

Seven years had passed since the Buddha's departure from his home in Kapilavastu. His father had sent many messengers to urge his son to return, but each group that had sought out the Buddha had forgotten its mission, been converted, and joined his ever-growing number of followers. But the Sakyamuni Buddha knew that eventually he must return home, even though he realized that the reunion would not be easy. King Suddhodhana had never forgiven his son for leaving. Prince Siddartha's wife had not given up hope that her husband would return to her, and the many members of the Sakya clan, uncles, cousins, and others, were sceptical about the Buddha's activities and achievements. The Buddha knew that no one is a prophet in his own land.

First of all, how would his clansmen receive him, they who had known him as a boy? It was necessary for all to bow down to the Buddha, but many were unwilling or full of doubt. So the Buddha performed a magical feat. He floated a platform in the air as high as the top of a Sal tree, and he greeted his clansmen from the platform. All eyes looked up to the Buddha, who then caused a rainstorm, allowing drops of water to fall on and cleanse only those who wished to be purified. The Sakyas admired and praised Sakyamuni for these achievements.

That night the Buddha slept in a park outside the city. The next morning he entered Kapilavastu with his bowl to beg for alms. Everyone saw him beg. The King was outraged and said it was a disgrace for the Prince, his son, to beg. The Buddha replied that it was his custom; Buddhas before him had gained their livelihood that way, and so would Buddhas of the future.

This was the day that Nanda the Fair, Sakyamuni's half-brother, was to be consecrated as heir to King Suddhodhana's throne and also the day that he was to be married. The Buddha went to Nanda and gave him his bowl to hold. He did not ask for it back, and because of Nanda's lifelong devotion, he was forced to follow the Buddha back to the monastic encampment. Nanda wanted desperately to return to his bride and his kingdom. But the Buddha wanted to show Nanda that his attachments to the world of illusion and suffering were meaningless. Therefore, he took Nanda to see the beauties of the firmament. They were so dazzling that he forgot his earthly longings and ultimately followed in the footsteps of the Buddha.

Seven days later Yasodhara, wife of Prince Siddartha, adorned her son Rahula with perfumed flowers and his finest robes. She instructed him to seek out the golden-coloured ascetic. She told Rahula that this holyman was his father and that Rahula should ask for his inheritance. Yasodhara told Rahula that his father had four great vases of treasure that Rahula would need to become heir to Suddhodhana's kingdom.)

Rahula went to his father and, as he had been instructed, he asked for his inheritance. But he was immediately consumed by a love for his father and followed him back to his retreat. There Rahula was welcomed and permitted to join the priestly order. The Buddha gave his son an exceptional inheritance, the great wealth of enlightenment.

Soon after this, King Suddhodhana died and Prajapati, mother of Nanda and foster mother of the Buddha, asked to join the Buddha's order. Women were not supposed to be admitted to this order and she was repeatedly rebuffed. Finally, however, the Buddha admitted this fiercely loyal and determined woman, who had shaved her head, assumed a monk's habit, and travelled with swollen, dust-covered feet.

In the years that followed, the Buddha wandered from village to village and taught all over India. He had many converts. One remarkable admirer was a monkey who offered him sweet, honey-like syrup that he collected from the tops of palm trees. Yet there continued to be many powerful sects competing with the Buddha. In fact, some leaders were jealous of his great following and wanted to discredit him. They challenged him to a contest at Sravasti to decide who preached the true doctrine. They talked, argued, and discussed. The Buddha demonstrated his superiority in this contest of words, but the great throngs of followers did not understand all that he said. The other contestants performed magical feats which appealed to the crowd more than words. The Buddha saw that if he was going to triumph over his rivals, he too would have to please the crowd. Once again, because he was the Buddha, he could break his own rule, which forbade monks to perform magic.

So it was that at Sravasti, he took a mango seed and planted it in the earth. Then he washed his hands over it. In just a few minutes, the seed sprouted into a seedling; it grew quickly into a sapling, and finally into a huge tree full of fruit and flowers with birds and bees buzzing happily among the leaves. The Buddha sat at the foot of its great trunk in the position of meditation. Suddenly, the Enlightened One was multiplied into ten thousand images which blanketed the cosmos. Then, he rose high above the tree to join these other images, and water and fire surged from his limbs.

After this spectacular feat, all the leaders of the rival schools and the throngs of viewers bowed down to the Buddha.

The monks practised their homeless life, wandering, never spending the night in the same place except during the rains of the monsoon season. They would then retreat to a rustic hut and meditate for three months. The Buddha Sakyamuni took this time to visit his mother, Queen Maya, in Tusita Heaven, a divine resting spot for the worthy, where she had been waiting for him to instruct her in his law. After three months had passed, he descended on a great golden stairway while the sky was filled with admiring gods who praised him and showered him with flowers.

The Buddha's cousin and childhood rival, Devadatta, had joined the order during the conversions at Kapilavastu, but his envious nature had not allowed him to comprehend the true path. As the years wore on and the Buddha's earthly tenure was drawing to a close, Devadatta wanted the leadership of the disciples for himself. The Buddha ignored him, and in a rage Devadatta plotted to kill the Buddha.

First, he hired archers to murder his cousin, but as they drew their bows, they froze in awe of the

Buddha's shining countenance. Their weapons fell to the earth, and they bowed down before the Buddha. So Devadatta himself tried to kill the Buddha. One day, while the Buddha walked to his place of meditation, he dropped a great rock from the mountain above him. The giant boulder plummeted down but, at the last moment, the gods intervened and diverted the rock so that only the Buddha's foot was hurt. Blood was drawn, but the wound was not serious. In a final effort, Devadatta obtained an elephant by bribing its keeper, made the elephant drunk, and loosed the mad beast in the Buddha's path to trample him in its drunken fury. But when the wild, foaming beast was confronted by Sakyamuni's radiance, it became subdued and fell to its knees in front of the Buddha. At that point, Devadatta ran away, but he immediately fell ill. He realized that his final hours had come, and he wanted to see the Sakyamuni again to beg his forgiveness. Since he was too weak to walk, he was carried to the Buddha, but the Buddha did not see him. As the litter approached the Buddha's retreat, the earth opened and Devadatta was swallowed up in a great chasm which led to Avici Hell. The pit was engulfed in flames and there was a stench of sulphur and burnt flesh. Here Devadatta would pay for his evil deeds, suffering there until he was reborn in the most miserable form of life such as a viper or a flea.

7. The Final Days

The Buddha Sakyamuni had preached his law for fifty years. He was now eighty. His body knew the infirmities of age and sickness. He was ready to pass on to his ultimate peace, *parinirvana*. He prepared to make his last journey. Before departure, he and his disciples were offered a meal of pork by a pious follower. Though the Buddha ate the meat, he forbade his disciples to eat it and warned his host to bury the rest of the meat. He said that only the Blessed One could digest this food. Yet even he could not. He became ill, but still insisted on beginning the journey. After they had walked several leagues, the Buddha, weak with fever, asked his faithful disciple Ananda to spread out his cloak so that he might rest, and then to bring him some water. Ananda told his master that five hundred carts had just crossed the nearby stream and the water would be churned up and muddy. Ananda suggested that they walk a little farther to a clear stream, where the master might both drink and bathe. But the Buddha insisted that Ananda bring him water near at hand. Ananda took the Buddha's bowl to the water that he was sure would be muddy, but he found it clear. Briefly refreshed, the group continued the journey, stopping twenty-four more times before arriving at the spot selected by the Buddha in a mango grove. The Buddha showed Ananda where to prepare his couch beneath a twin-trunked Sal tree and specified that his head face north. He told Ananda that he was weary and would lie down, and so he did, on his right side with one leg resting on the other and his right hand folded under his head.

The Buddha's disciple wept and told his master that he should not leave him without teaching all that he must know. The Buddha reminded him that all who are born must die, and that if Ananda practised the great law, he too would eventually

be free to enter *nirvana*. He then sent Ananda to
the city to inform the King and the people that
the Buddha was dying, so that they could come
and bid him farewell. The site where the Buddha
lay down to die was in the country of Mallas. All
the Malla tribesmen wished to see the Buddha before he died, so the disciples helped to arrange au-
diences one family at a time. Others heard the
news and rushed to see the Buddha before it was
too late. Thousands of years had passed waiting
for the Buddha and many thousands more would
pass before the next Buddha would come.

The night was almost over, and so too was the
Buddha's existence. Knowing this, he called his
disciples before him and reminded them that "As
creation begins in dust so it returns to dust" and
that they should work hard towards salvation.
After these words, the Blessed One passed into a
series of trances, death overtook his limbs, and he
attained his ultimate peace, *parinirvana*. He had,
through his seeking, lifted the veil of ignorance
and revealed the illusory nature of life. He had
preached detachment from this illusion, which
would allow a person to escape *samsara*, the endless cycle of rebirth and suffering, and to arrive
at *nirvana*.

The Buddha was dead. All his disciples and all
the Malla tribesmen gathered around his death

bed and wept. According to custom his body was placed on a great pyre and consumed in flames. His ashes remained and were to be buried, along with other relics such as his bowl and cloak, beneath a sacred mound.

The Mallas were proud that the Buddha had attained his final peace in their land, leaving them his sacred relics. But the neighbouring kingdoms where the Buddha had wandered and preached also claimed the relics. Eight different tribes were on the brink of a holy war to fight for these relics when the matter was turned over to a sage Brahman, who divided the relics into eight equal parts. Each part was taken to a place which had been important during the Buddha's life, places where he had preached and performed miracles. On each site a mound was built as a shrine for the relics, a memorial to the Buddha who found the way to end suffering in the world.

Glossary

Ananda : Sakyamuni Buddha's favourite disciple.

ascetic : A person who has renounced possessions and worldly ties to practise a religious life. He wanders, with forests and deserts as his home, undergoing privation and hardship. He believes this life will lead to understanding and wisdom.

Asita: Holyman who forecasts Siddartha's Buddahood.

Avici Hell: A monstrous place where evil people go and suffer, to pay for the sins of their former lives.

Bodhi Tree. [Bo Tree]: Tree of enlightenment The tree under which Gotama the Ascetic sat for fifty days until he reached his enlightenment and became the Buddha.

Brahmanic sects: Schools of religion following the old order of Indian worship.

Buddha; The Enlightened One: One who under-
stands the causes of man's suffering and is
able to stop suffering through righteous acts
and detachment. Through this enlightenment
or new understanding he attains *nirvana*,
which is the end of suffering.

Devadatta: Cousin to Siddartha, and his jealous
rival.

eightfold path: The Buddha's prescription for attaining enlightenment which leads to *nirvana*
(salvation) : Think right thoughts, say right
words and perform right deeds, have right
aspirations and intentions, live the right ways
of life, perform right efforts and meditations.

Enlightened One: The Buddha.

enlightenment: Achieving understanding of the
causes of suffering, and how to escape it. Per-
ceiving the illusory nature of life within the
cycle of recurring births, and realizing that
man is a transient, perishable, replaceable
being, as unimportant as a grain of sand at
the bottom of a vast ocean. Understanding
that man's passionate attachment to this life
brings on this suffering, whereas detachment
from life can lead to peace.

four noble truths: The nature of the universe as
explained by the Buddha:

1. *All of life is suffering,* from birth to death.
2. A person suffers because he clings to the deception that he is something important and permanent, when in fact he is insignificant, mortal, and replaceable. *As long as man clings to this false illusion of life, he will suffer.*
3. To escape suffering, one must escape from the cycle of rebirth by *detaching oneself from the passions of life.*
4. Buddha's prescription for salvation; avoid suffering by *following the eightfold path: think right thoughts, say right words, perform right deeds, have right aspirations and intentions, live the right ways of life, perform right efforts and meditations.*

Gotama the Ascetic: The name Siddartha adopts after he leaves his family and kingdom to lead a homeless life in search of a way to cure man's suffering. (Gotama, Pali spelling of name; Gautama, Sanskrit spelling of name.)

Kasyapa: A holy man, leader of a Brahmanic sect that worshipped the old gods of India.

King Suddhodhana: Ruler of the Sakya Kingdom; husband of Queen Maya; father of Siddartha.

lotus: The flower used to symbolize the Buddha's purity amidst a corrupt world of passion and suffering. The lotus grows in a swamp, yet it is a clean and perfect flower unaffected by its surroundings. The lotus also suggests the cycle of birth, death, and rebirth since it re-seeds itself in the swamp.

Mara: God of evil and constant tempter of the Buddha. He is the personification of man's passionate attachment to life.

middle way: Course of life prescribed by the Buddha : one should not indulge oneself excessively either in pleasure or in pain. Follow a central path, avoiding extremes.

muni: Sage, monk.

naga: Serpent.

Nanda the Fair: Son of Prajapati and King Suddhodhana and half-brother of Siddartha. He becomes heir to King Suddhodhana's throne after Siddartha's renunciation.

nirvana: The stateless state; the peace to be found at the cessation of recurring births; the end of suffering; salvation.

parinirvana: The state into which the Buddha passes at death; his ultimate peace.

Prajapati (Mayaprajapati) : Aunt and foster-mother to Siddartha; mother of Nanda; sister to Queen Maya; wife of King Suddhodhana.

Prince Siddartha: Child of Queen Maya and King Suddhodhana (King of the Sakyas) ; destined to be the Buddha.

Queen Maya (Mahamaya): Wife of King Suddhodhana; mother of Siddartha.

Rahula: Son of Prince Siddartha and Yasodhara.

renunciation: Giving up the luxury of a home
and possessions and the pleasure and ties of
family and the right to inheritance. Going
into the world with nothing but oneself, living like a hermit, and begging for food. Siddartha gave up his luxurious life, possessions,
family, and kingdom, to wander as an ascetic.

Rose-apple tree: The tree under which Siddartha
sat in his first meditation at the ploughing
festival when he was thirteen years old.

Rudraka: A holyman who taught Gotama the
Ascetic religious discipline.

Sakya: Family name of King Suddhodhana and
Prince Siddartha.

Sakyamuni Buddha: Gotama the Ascetic's name
after he finds enlightenment. It means sage of
the Sakya clan.

Sal tree: Many events important to the Buddha
occur near this type of tree. It is the tree that
bent down its branch for Queen Maya to hold
when she gave birth to Siddartha.

salvation: The end of suffering; *nirvana.*

samsara: The endless cycle of rebirth. One is
born, dies, and is reborn—the inevitable life
pattern. To be reborn is to suffer.

Tusita Heaven: The place where Queen Maya resides waiting to be reborn in her next existence. Deserving people wait there for rebirth while enjoying its celestial beauty.

vina: A musical instrument with seven strings, a fretted finger board, and a gourd at each end.

wheel of law: The doctrine or prescription for salvation preached by the Buddha. When the Buddha preached his law, he began to set the wheel of law into motion.

Yasodhara: Wife of Prince Siddartha; mother of Rahula.

Epilogue

Understanding and respecting cultures other than our own is essential if we are to create a harmonious world community. The story of the Buddha offers an exciting way to begin to penetrate Asian thought. Buddhist doctrine expresses a set of values and a view of the universe very different from those underlying Western thought. For over two thousand years, Buddhism has been a vital religious movement in Asia and it continues to be a major force there today. The sites where the Buddha preached in his lifetime are still revered. Buddhists make pilgrimages to Bodhgaya, the place of enlightenment, and also to the Deer Park in Sarnath, where the Buddha preached his first sermon. But because Hinduism and Mohammedanism eclipsed Buddhism in the later periods in India, little of the glory of the Buddha remains in that country today. Buddhism, which began to decline in India in about the 6th century A.D., survived longer in the border regions and now only remains tucked away in the Himalayas. However, gifted and energetic monks had taken the golden image and the Buddha's law to China, Japan, and Southeast Asia, where they achieved unprecedented success. It is in these countries that the dynamism of that religion is felt today.

The Buddha was an historic figure, the son of an elected chief of the Sakya clan, born in the sixth century before Christ in what is now Nepal. The concept of his royal lineage is part of the myth that has grown up about the Buddha. We do know that he left his kingdom to preach his version of salvation in northern India from the Himalayas to the Ganges River basin. There are no contemporary accounts of the Buddha's life and teaching. The earliest accounts were written at least several hundred years after his death. Dim memories and embellishments have formed various versions of his life. In sacred texts stating the Buddha's law, isolated incidents of his life were told as parables, or episodes, appeared written in marginal commentaries. The first complete version of the life was inserted in an old text in about the fourth century A.D., approximately eight hundred years after the death of the Buddha. Thus we have a variety of different versions of any given episode or sequence of events, and the details of these stories vary with the time, region, and language in which they were written.

I have selected from this rich literature the most often told events of the Buddha's life and have tried to organize them into a coherent story, hoping to combine the magic of the myth with the basic ideas of the Buddha's teaching. Though we recognize the historical fact of the Buddha's person, most of the details of his biography are submerged in the myth. Somewhere within this beautiful tale is the truth of his life.

Many works were consulted in the preparation of this book. Listed here are only the major sources on which I have drawn.

BURLINGAME, EUGENE WATSON. *Buddhist Legends*. Translated from the original Pali text of Dhammapada Commentary. Harvard Oriental Series. Vols. 28, 29, 30. Cambridge, Mass: Harvard University Press, 1921.

FOUCHER, A. *The Life of the Buddha*. Translated from the French by Simone Brangier Boas. Connecticut: Wesleyan University Press, 1963.

JOHNSON, E. H. *The Buddhacarita*. A translation from the original Sanskrit of Asvaghosa, supplemented by the Tibeton version. Calcutta: Baptist Mission Press, 1936.

LAMOTTE, ETIENNE. *Histoire du Bouddhisme Indien*. Belgium: Université de Louvain, 1958.

THOMAS, EDWARD J. *The Life of the Buddha*. London: Routledge & Kegan Paul Ltd., 1956.

I wish to thank Mrs. Sissela Bok and her daughter Hilary for their interest, which initiated this book. I want to thank Professor John Rosenfield as well for bibliographical help and invaluable suggestions on the manuscript. I also wish to thank Miss Thalia Kennedy and Mrs. Angelica Rudenstine of the Boston Museum of Fine Arts, and Mrs. Bert Neustadt and my husband, Jerome Alan Cohen, for their help. In addition, I am grateful to Mrs. Merloyd Lawrence for her illuminating editorial suggestions which should ensure her a high place on Mt. Sumeru in the Buddhist pantheon.